Acting Edition

Off Off Broadway Festival Plays, 46th Series

By Grace (Part Two)
by Agyeiwaa Asante

Kitchen Design
by Suzanne Willett

pearl apple penguin
by Aisling Towl

Grieved.
by Jahquale Mazyck

Dogs of Society
by Julia Grogan

All Things Considered...
by A.J. Ditty

SAMUEL FRENCH

By Grace (Part Two) © 2021 by Agyeiwaa Asante
Kitchen Design © 2021 by Suzanne Willett
pearl apple penguin © 2021 by Aisling Towl
Grieved. © 2021 by Jahquale Mazyck
Dogs of Society © 2021 by Julia Grogan
All Things Considered... © 2021 by A.J. Ditty
All Rights Reserved

OFF OFF BROADWAY FESTIVAL PLAYS, 46TH SERIES is fully protected under the copyright laws of the United States of America, the British Commonwealth, including Canada, and all member countries of the Berne Convention for the Protection of Literary and Artistic Works, the Universal Copyright Convention, and/or the World Trade Organization conforming to the Agreement on Trade Related Aspects of Intellectual Property Rights. All rights, including professional and amateur stage productions, recitation, lecturing, public reading, motion picture, radio broadcasting, television, online/digital production, and the rights of translation into foreign languages are strictly reserved.

ISBN 978-0-573-70969-2

www.concordtheatricals.com
www.concordtheatricals.co.uk

FOR PRODUCTION INQUIRIES

UNITED STATES AND CANADA
info@concordtheatricals.com
1-866-979-0447

UNITED KINGDOM AND EUROPE
licensing@concordtheatricals.co.uk
020-7054-7298

Each title is subject to availability from Concord Theatricals Corp., depending upon country of performance. Please be aware that *OFF OFF BROADWAY FESTIVAL PLAYS, 46TH SERIES* may not be licensed by Concord Theatricals Corp. in your territory. Professional and amateur producers should contact the nearest Concord Theatricals Corp. office or licensing partner to verify availability.

CAUTION: Professional and amateur producers are hereby warned that *OFF OFF BROADWAY FESTIVAL PLAYS, 46TH SERIES* is subject to a licensing fee. The purchase, renting, lending or use of this book does not constitute a license to perform this title(s), which license must be obtained from Concord Theatricals Corp. prior to any performance. Performance of this title(s) without a license is a violation of federal law and may subject the producer and/or presenter of such performances to civil penalties. Both amateurs and professionals considering a production are strongly advised to apply to the appropriate agent before starting rehearsals, advertising, or booking a theatre. A licensing fee must be paid whether the title(s) is presented for charity or gain and whether or not admission is charged. Professional/Stock licensing fees are quoted upon application to Concord Theatricals Corp.

This work is published by Samuel French, an imprint of Concord Theatricals Corp.

No one shall make any changes in this title(s) for the purpose of production. No part of this book may be reproduced, stored in a retrieval system, scanned, uploaded, or transmitted in any form, by any means, now known or yet to be invented, including mechanical, electronic, digital, photocopying, recording, videotaping, or otherwise, without the prior written permission of the publisher. No one shall share this title(s), or any part of this title(s), through any social media or file hosting websites.

For all inquiries regarding motion picture, television, online/digital and other media rights, please contact Concord Theatricals Corp.

MUSIC AND THIRD-PARTY MATERIALS USE NOTE

Licensees are solely responsible for obtaining formal written permission from copyright owners to use copyrighted music and/or other copyrighted third-party materials (e.g., artworks, logos) in the performance of this play and are strongly cautioned to do so. If no such permission is obtained by the licensee, then the licensee must use only original music and materials that the licensee owns and controls. Licensees are solely responsible and liable for clearances of all third-party copyrighted materials, including without limitation music, and shall indemnify the copyright owners of the play(s) and their licensing agent, Concord Theatricals Corp., against any costs, expenses, losses and liabilities arising from the use of such copyrighted third-party materials by licensees. For music, please contact the appropriate music licensing authority in your territory for the rights to any incidental music.

IMPORTANT BILLING AND CREDIT REQUIREMENTS

If you have obtained performance rights to this title, please refer to your licensing agreement for important billing and credit requirements.

Concord Theatricals presents The Samuel French Off Off Broadway Short Play Festival (OOB) has been the nation's leading short play festival for forty-six years. The OOB Festival has served as a doorway to future success for aspiring writers. Over 200 plays have been published, and many participants have become established, award-winning playwrights.

For more information on the Off Off Broadway Short Play Festival, including history, interviews, and more, please visit www.oobfestival.com.

Festival Sponsor: Concord Theatricals

Festival Artistic Director: Casey McLain
Literary Director: Garrett Anderson
Client Manager: Abbie Van Nostrand
Festival Moderator: Amy Rose Marsh
Marketing Team: Jeremiah Hernandez, Courtney Kochuba, Imogen Lloyd Webber
Festival Staff / Readers: Rosemary Bucher, Charlie Coulthard, Billie Davis, Sean Demers, Sequoyah Douglas, Fiona Kyle, Rachel Levens, Debbie McLean, Tyler Mullen, Nate Netzley, Alex Perez, Meg Schadl, Rachel Smith

HONORARY GUEST PLAYWRIGHT
Heidi Schreck

FESTIVAL JUDGES
Dennis A Allen II
Nan Barnett
Miranda Rose Hall
Trish Harnetiaux
Zora Howard
Margaret Ledford
Harrison David Rivers
Jeremy Stoller
Susi Westfall

TABLE OF CONTENTS

Foreword vii

By Grace (Part Two) 1
by Agyeiwaa Asante

Kitchen Design... 17
by Suzanne Willett

pearl apple penguin..33
by Aisling Towl

Grieved.. 51
by Jahquale Mazyck

Dogs of Society..69
by Julia Grogan

All Things Considered......................................99
by A.J. Ditty

FOREWORD

Concord Theatricals is honored to have the six daring and inspirational playwrights included in this collection as the winners of our 46th Annual Off Off Broadway Short Play Festival. This year our Festival received over 750 submissions from around the world. We thank all of these gifted playwrights for sharing their talent with us and welcome each writer into our elite group of Off Off Broadway Festival winners.

When we sat down to plan our 46th consecutive year of the OOB Festival, our team recognized that some changes would have to take place due to the continued complications of the COVID-19 pandemic. However, we found it reassuring to reflect on our past festivals, which have ranged in evaluation format and performance presentation.

For the second year in a row, to ensure the safety and well-being of everyone involved, we removed the performance aspect and went back to our roots by choosing the six winners through reading evaluation only. We missed our extended OOB Festival theatre family – the actors, directors, stage managers, and tech crews – but we were excited to focus directly upon that which the festival was built: the script and the playwright.

From our initial pool of Top-Thirty playwrights, we ultimately select six plays for publication and representation by Concord Theatricals. Of course, we can't make our selections alone, so we enlist some brilliant minds within the theatre industry to help us in this process. We invited an esteemed group of nine judges consisting of a mix of Concord Theatricals playwrights and members of the theatre industry. We thank them for their support, insight, and commitment to the art of playwriting.

Concord Theatricals is the world's most significant theatrical company, comprising the catalogs of R&H Theatricals, Samuel French, Tams-Witmark, and The Andrew Lloyd Webber Collection. We are constantly striving to develop groundbreaking methods that will better connect playwright and producer. With a team committed to continuing our tradition of publishing and licensing the best new theatrical works, we are boldly embracing our role in this industry as bridge between playwright and theatre.

On behalf of the entire Concord Theatricals team in our New York, London, and Berlin offices, and the over 10,000 playwrights, composers, and lyricists that we publish and represent, we present you with the six winning plays of the 46th Annual Samuel French Off Off Broadway Short Play Festival.

This festival is about playwrights. Sharing the human story. We invite you to enjoy these extraordinary plays.

Casey McLain
Artistic Director
The Samuel French Off Off Broadway Short Play Festival

By Grace (Part Two)

Agyeiwaa Asante

CHARACTERS

AYAA – (she/her) twenties, light-skinned and/or bi-racial woman of African ancestry.

JOYCE – (she/her) twenties, brown or dark-skinned woman of African ancestry.

SETTING

Metropolitan city. Abortion Clinic.

TIME

Post "post-racial" America.

To all the Black girls figuring it out, just like me.

(**TWO YOUNG BLACK WOMEN** *sit in a waiting room. The kind that's trying too hard, yet not at all, to look comforting. These women are roommates, friends, a support system.* **JOYCE** *mechanically flips through a magazine.* **AYAA**, *on the other hand, can't seem to sit still.*)

AYAA. Planned Parenthood is really nice. Like it's such a *good* thing. I should donate.

JOYCE. I think we're doing our part keeping the doors open.

AYAA. I've been thinking about that, donating? If I do it enough? Like I do that round up thing at the grocery store even though I heard it's kind of a scam. But I do give money on Patreon so that goes like, directly to the artists?

JOYCE. I'm sure Issa Rae appreciates your two dollars a month.

AYAA. I'm supporting a creative I admire!

JOYCE. You do it for the exclusive videos and shit. Is it really donating if you're getting something out of it?

AYAA. Doesn't the one percent do that with like, tax-deductible donations?

JOYCE. True.

AYAA. Like Bill Gates doesn't really give a shit about the kids in Africa getting Surface Pros, you know?

But Planned Parenthood, this place is nice. Useful too. Like, helpful. I should give something.

JOYCE. You do that, just shut up and sit still, please. You're making everyone uncomfortable.

AYAA. Who everyone? It's eight in the morning on a Tuesday. What, you don't think the receptionist lady knows what's going down?

JOYCE. [I'm] not watching you do somersaults in that chair!

(AYAA *sits. Beat.*)

AYAA. I think you should call him now.

JOYCE. No.

AYAA. *OR* just like send him a text or something, just so he knows?

JOYCE. I will tell him, if I *decide* to tell him, *after*. When I know it's taken care of.

AYAA. That's kind of messed up.

JOYCE. *"My body, my choice."* Remember?

AYAA. I'm not saying it isn't. Not saying a nigga gets a vote, but he should at least be *informed*.

JOYCE. He's literally not even.

AYAA. *Fine.* Your Caucasian suitor should have knowledge of the events that are about to transpire. And he's not even like that! He'd totally support you. Hell, he'd pay for it, driven you up here, rub your feet when they're up in the little stirrups –

JOYCE. I. Said. *No.*

AYAA. *Okayyyyyy.*

(JOYCE *holds her stomach, groans a little.*)

Are you okay? Do you need me to get you something?

JOYCE. No, I think it's just because I didn't eat anything.

AYAA. Were you not supposed to?

JOYCE. I don't remember, probably not, right? I didn't feel like it anyway. I felt too...

>   (*Pause.*)

AYAA. Y'all woulda made a cute baby.

JOYCE. OMG, can you *not*.

AYAA. What? I'm just saying, you're cute, he's cute, I'd be a great auntie –

JOYCE. Keep your bi-racial fantasies out of my uterus.

AYAA. *No*, I mean like your *features* as two cute *people*.

JOYCE. Like?

AYAA. You know like, the nose –

JOYCE. His.

AYAA. The eyes –

JOYCE. Hazel –

AYAA. The hair –

JOYCE. Like yours.

AYAA. Joyceeeeahhhh! It can still look like you.

>   (*Pause.*)

JOYCE. He would make a good daddy, I think.

AYAA. He's already got the dad jokes.

JOYCE. And he wears Christmas sweaters, like, all the time. What is that? Argyle?

>   (*They laugh.*)

AYAA. Do you think you love him?

JOYCE. I think I like him a lot. Love feels kinda strong for a couple months?

AYAA. Is it?

JOYCE. I don't know. Isn't it?

AYAA. I just always feel like it just hits. When it hits you, you know. You know?

JOYCE. Well, it doesn't matter anyway.

(**AYAA** *gives a quizzical look.*)

['Cause] I'm breaking up with him, dafaq?

AYAA. Wait, over this? You're breaking up with him over this???

JOYCE. This was like a literal sign, neon lights and everything, from GOD. I shouldn't have been messing with him in the first place!

AYAA. No, this was a sign you shouldn't have unprotected sex between birth control methods, ya horny bitch.

JOYCE. It was *spur of the moment.*

AYAA. An impromptu trip over the Caucasus mountains?

JOYCE. Shut up!

AYAA. Wow, your very first white guy. And he gets you pregnant.

JOYCE. UGH.

AYAA. Let the colonizer in, and the seeds of imperialism are sewn –

JOYCE. *Shut up.*

AYAA. – into your uterus.

JOYCE. CAN YOU NOT.

AYAA. I'm sorry, it's funny as fuck!

JOYCE. This is my life, Ayaa! I can't be doin' stupid shit like this! I'm literally in the middle of a friggin' degree that I'm paying out the ass for. We're not kids anymore!

AYAA. I know, that's why I thought you'd be happy.

JOYCE. And how'd you figure that?

AYAA. I just thought we'd gotten to that part in our lives where this is good news. Where you say, "Congratulations!" not "Oh shit, what are you gonna do, your mom is going to kill you!"

JOYCE. My mom *would* still kill me.

AYAA. That's just 'cause you're not married. It's different now, we're adults. You're getting a Master's degree! You have a job! You always said you could see yourself being a mom.

JOYCE. Wrong person, wrong time.

AYAA. Because he's not the One? Or 'cause he's the *white* one?

JOYCE. Look, I have a plan. You *know* the plan. Master's, promotion, house, then on the eve of my twenty-ninth birthday find my Blackass bae, have a Blackass wedding, have two Blackass kids, and that's life!

AYAA. This whole "Blackass" theme is new.

JOYCE. I never thought I had to specify until now. It's just what I want, how I *imagined* it. Everyone has... preferences. And I know, that's like a dangerous word because people use it as an excuse to be racist and transphobic and shit, but as a racial minority –

AYAA. Well globally speaking we're [the majority] –

JOYCE. *I mean in this country*, my preference isn't rooted in hatred or bigotry or whatever. It's actually more like...preservation. Of one's culture.

AYAA. Your womb is going to preserve the culture? Like some kind of Black Virgin Mary?

JOYCE. Ain't nobody said nothin' about a savior, but like, it happens all the time. Languages, stories, customs.

They all get lost if you don't do your part to preserve them. I only have so much control over that, and so much of that is in the family I raise.

AYAA. Seriously?

JOYCE. Seriously.

AYAA. That's the most hotep thing I've ever heard you say.

JOYCE. Now that can't be true. Think of it like the Twitter memes? Of bi-racial kids with white moms?

AYAA. The ones with the asymmetrical side bang?

JOYCE. And their son's name is always some version of "Jayden" with a lot of *Y*s in it?

AYAA. And the daughter's called Jada or Naveh?

JOYCE. And they act like Drake?

AYAA. Or think they're Obama?

JOYCE. Exactlyyyy.

(They laugh.)

AYAA. But that's my point, you're not that.

JOYCE. I know, but that shit's a slippery slope.

AYAA. You wouldn't let that happen.

JOYCE. It doesn't matter either way 'cause whatever is in here, it's coming out.

(She pushes on her abdomen again as if to quiet a rumbling.)

AYAA. Look, we are both firmly pro-choice feminists, so that's not the question. But you having this abortion just 'cause this kid is gonna be half-white is messed up. It'd still be *yours*, isn't that what matters?

JOYCE. That's not the reason *why* I'm doing it. I'm twenty-seven and live in a studio apartment with you! *You* who survives by selling her mixed media art on Twitter. I am not in the frame of *life* to be having a child right now.

AYAA. But if Connor was a 6'2" thick-bearded brother from the motherland, you're saying you wouldn't hesitate? Some John Boyega – T'Challa type – dude?

JOYCE. I would still hesitate because I wouldn't want to end up like one of those podcast listener letters.

AYAA. *"Dear Kid Fury and Crissle –"*

JOYCE. *"– I met this great guy. He's super sweet, really handsome. The only problem is – "*

AYAA. *"– one of his baby mommas has me on a hitlist, he hasn't paid rent in two months and I haven't orgasmed in five."* Oh shit, *The Read* comes out today!

JOYCE. I think it's internalized xenophobia. That doesn't sound right. Nationalism? Like intense Black Power Pride.

AYAA. Does that make it better?

JOYCE. I know the right answer is no, but also… I don't think I care?

AYAA. *(Mock shock.)* Are you your own problematic fav?

JOYCE. And, truth? I think I'm okay with it.

AYAA. *Wooow.*

  (Pause.)

So I'm going to say this –

JOYCE. Or you could just not.

AYAA. So do you like… Do you see me as the enemy? Maybe not like THE enemy, but like *a* enemy?

JOYCE. Oh hell.

AYAA. I'm just asking! Not trying to take this personally –

JOYCE. Shouldn't remotely be that hard.

AYAA. But it's like, the revolution is going on out there. And people are doing crazy shit like Dolezaling and blackfishing – there were, like three college professors last month who got exposed for pretending to be POC! And people are upset, and rightly so, but now there's suddenly like all this…gatekeeping.

JOYCE. Okay, no one has ever called you, or confused you, for white a day in your life.

AYAA. No, but I'm bi-racial now.

JOYCE. *Now?*

AYAA. Not like now, as in "suddenly," but I've literally had people correct me!

JOYCE. I told you to stay offa Facebook.

AYAA. I'm serious! Someone retweeted me saying buying my art isn't supporting a black owned business.

JOYCE. It's *hardly* a business –

AYAA. Joyceaahhh!

JOYCE. What? You won't even set up a PayPal! CashApping to $PiscesPrincess93 is hardly professional. Besides, I'm the only hotep you should be listening to, remember? And you're black and bi-racial, you get to be both.

AYAA. Exactly! That's the problem I'm like, on both sides! Which means I'm not on any side and you can't trust someone who's not on any side.

JOYCE. There isn't a literal race war, stop talking about sides! If you were so fucking problematic, I wouldn't tolerate you.

AYAA. So, you trust me?

JOYCE. Yes, I trust you.

AYAA. Even if you resent me sometimes?

JOYCE. I don't resent you. But it's a real light-skin trait to make this about you right now.

I resent the world that considers you better than me, but no, not you. You are not *the* enemy or *my* enemy or *an* enemy. You are just you. Stay that way.

> (**JOYCE** *rubs at her stomach again, uncomfortable.* **AYAA** *looks at her.*)

BITCH. WHAT.

AYAA. So, hypothetically –

JOYCE. Hell.

AYAA. What if you could only have one baby and this was it. Would you still keep it?

JOYCE. Ayaa. What the fuck.

AYAA. If this was your only opportunity to become a mom.

JOYCE. First of all, no. There are a bunch of ways to become a parent. I'm up for being a foster parent, adopt one day.

AYAA. Just answer the question.

JOYCE. …Yes, okay! Damn.

AYAA. Or are you just saying that 'cause anything else you'd say would be fucked up?

JOYCE. You think everything I say is fucked up why would I start censoring myself now?

AYAA. So what would make it so bad? To have a little off-white to caramel little person?

JOYCE. Off-white?

AYAA. The Mariah Carey – TiaTamara Mowry bi-racial spectrum.

JOYCE. The problem is if it's a girl.

AYAA. Ouch.

JOYCE. Not. About. You.

Look, being a woman, it's fucked up as it is. It's hard AF. So she's already gonna have it hard. Then she's gonna be some version of black, so that's another one. Two strikes. THEN I'm also gonna have to explain to her that she has light skin privilege? That even though for all the above reasons she has it bad, I also have to explain how it's not as bad? Because I'll be DAMNED if I raise anyone who's gonna run around this planet claiming colorism doesn't exist. Or worse, that reverse colorism does.

AYAA. That Alexandra Shipp interview was *so bad*. Are we ever getting a dark-skinned Storm?

JOYCE. I just want to raise a little brown skin girl, if that's how they identify, just like me. But better. Not that she'd have to be better, she'd just have it that way. A version that'll never want to perm her hair and who will always play in the sun. Who'll wear little t-shirts that say "Flexin' My Complexions" and "Melanin Magic." Who won't have a single Disney Princess that looks like her, but a dozen.

I think I just want a do-over.

And it'd just be different, okay? It'd just be different. The whole world is gonna be beige by 2075 anyway. I just want to raise one little dark-skinned girl who's gonna know that of all the things that could be wrong with her, the color on her skin isn't one of them. That's, like, the part of my legacy I want to leave, okay?

(Beat.)

And if it's a boy, I'll teach him to be non-toxic. Not to have his masculinity be his defining trait. That it's okay to love, whoever he wants to love, and that includes himself. And that it's no one's job to do it for him.

(Beat.)

And if they live outside the fuckin' binary, then I just want that baby to live. Like unhindered, unlimited... I get we can't control how our kids are going to turn out or whatever, and there's like the ethics of designer babies and you should just love your kids no matter what, and I'd love this one no matter what, even if I walked out of this place right now. But right now, it's not. It's not a child and I don't owe it anything. Life is hard enough as it is to just be brought into the world just because.

> *(Pause. They sit. A pained expression grows on their faces.)*
>
> *(**JOYCE** looks down, touches between her legs. She brings her hand out. Blood.)*

AYAA. Oh.

JOYCE. *(Unemotional.)* Fuck.

End of Play

Kitchen Design

Suzanne Willett

CHARACTERS

WOMAN 1 – F, 30s-50s, proper
WOMAN 2 – F, 30s-50s, conforming
WOMAN 3 – F, 30s-50s, conflicted
TWO STAGEHANDS – M/F, 30s-50s

SETTING

A kitchen. Woman 1 seems to be in a different kitchen than Woman 2 and Woman 3.

TIME

Presentish

Scene One
How to Redecorate Your Kitchen

>*(A kitchen. Pastels. Proper etiquette and proper bearing.* **WOMAN 1** *stands in the center of a kitchen. At two tables and two chairs on opposite sides of the stage sit* **WOMAN 2** *and* **WOMAN 3***. They sip tea from a cup and saucer. Cups are set down with a faint clink.)*

WOMAN 1. The kitchen is an important place in every home. Here, families stand beside each other after a long and tedious day. To ensure that you enjoy spending time in the kitchen, make it look presentable and impressive. Remarkably, by redecorating the kitchen space, it will look bigger and better and you will opt to spend most of your time there.

There are many benefits to upgrading and/or redecorating your kitchen. Of course, you've got your aesthetic benefits: who doesn't love a nice, visually appealing upgrade?

WOMAN 2. I'm all about kitchen gadgets.

WOMAN 1. But as you start to plan out your renovation efforts, you'll learn that there are several other benefits, too. For example, simple changes to your kitchen's storage capacity and layout can make your space much more functional.

WOMAN 3. I'm all about gadgets that are versatile, high performing and easy to use.

>*(They sip. Lights fade. Sounds of dishes being put on the table. This goes on for awhile with clinks and clashes.)*

Scene Two
Brighten Up the Kitchen

> (*A low light reveals* **WOMAN 2** *and* **WOMAN 3**'s *table covered with dishes. Reds, blues, 1970s amber, green, a hodgepodge of ceramic throughout the ages. The light rises.*)

WOMAN 1. A dark kitchen will feel smaller than it actually is. However, brightening it up will have a very huge impact. In case you don't want to change the color of your walls and cabinets, you can alternatively add different lighting types. Using under the cabinet lighting will accent the cabinets while at the same time brightening the work area.

> (**WOMAN 2** *begins to stack the dishes. It is a louder clanging.* **WOMAN 1** *approves.*)

WOMAN 2. (*To* **WOMAN 1.**) What is the one household item

WOMAN 1. Regardless of the color, good lighting will make the room feel bigger and cozier.

> (**WOMAN 3** *stacks.*)

WOMAN 3. the one

WOMAN 1. Some lighting ideas you can consider include:

WOMAN 2. the one you use the most

WOMAN 1. Adding LED lights on the shelves and the area below your cabinets, this will help illuminate the counter space.

WOMAN 2. (*Impatiently.*) the one household item you use

WOMAN 3. with two kids

WOMAN 2. a dog

WOMAN 3. and a husband

(**WOMAN 2** *stops stacking. To* **WOMAN 3***: So, what's the one?*)

WOMAN 1. Replacing incandescent light bulbs with the modern energy efficient versions. Clipping pendant lights on the existing lighting system which helps layer the room's lighting.

WOMAN 2. the one

WOMAN 3. the one?

WOMAN 1. \ Replacing outdated light fixtures.

WOMAN 2. you use the most

WOMAN 1. or adding a mirror to the kitchen wall will help reflect the light.

WOMAN 2. paper towels!

WOMAN 3. paper towels

WOMAN 2 & WOMAN 3. cleans up the mess!

(**WOMAN 2** *and* **WOMAN 3** *stack. Sounds of ceramic.*)

Scene Three
Highlight Color

(**WOMAN 2** *and* **WOMAN 3** *begin to stack the dishes faster, in any random order. A separation of the space begins.* **WOMAN 1** *remains in the kitchen, becoming irritated.*)

WOMAN 1. With modern kitchen designs, it is easy to enjoy creativity

WOMAN 3. holiday party

WOMAN 1. when it comes to interior decoration.

WOMAN 2. party days

WOMAN 1. You can use creative designs

WOMAN 2. in what clothes

WOMAN 1. to redecorate your kitchen walls such as colorful intertwined stripes.

WOMAN 2. pajamas anyway

WOMAN 3. clothes party in wine

WOMAN 1. This will not only make the room appear larger

WOMAN 3. party days

WOMAN 1. but also introduce bright colors

WOMAN 2. happy anyway

(**WOMAN 2** *looks at* **WOMAN 3**: *Get with the program.*)

WOMAN 1. more elegant

WOMAN 2. (*Irritated.*) day three

WOMAN 1. brighter

WOMAN 2. (*To* **WOMAN 2.**) *day three*

WOMAN 1. and fun to spend time in.

WOMAN 3. three happy –

WOMAN 2. Make peace with it

WOMAN 3. same day

WOMAN 2. Make peace with it

WOMAN 3. chocolate with myself

    cookie room

    same procedure

    days locked

    myself chipped

    room three

    holiday in a party

Scene Four
Use Ceramic Decoration as a Highlight

>(**WOMAN 2** *and* **3** *stack the dishes faster.* **WOMAN 1** *moves to the ceramic tile backsplash.*)

WOMAN 1. Ceramic tiles come in many designs which provide endless possibilities for customizing your kitchen.

WOMAN 2. I'm happy to announce holiday pajamas

WOMAN 1. Ceramic tiles are durable such that when cutlery falls on it doesn't scratch.

WOMAN 3. I'm announcing happy holiday pajamas

WOMAN 1. These tile designs are also able to withstand frequent traffic

WOMAN 2. Pajamas announcing I'm happy

WOMAN 1. they don't absorb odors

WOMAN 2. happy holiday party hosting

WOMAN 1. and may have a finish that makes them slip resistant

WOMAN 3. happy party announcing

>(**WOMAN 3** *grabs a dish and holds it over her head.* **WOMAN 2** *looks at* **WOMAN 3**: *Don't.*)

(Sarcastically.) Make peace with it

WOMAN 2. Make peace with it

WOMAN 3. Make sense of it

WOMAN 2. Make sure of it

WOMAN 3. Make shit of it

>(**WOMAN 3** *smashes the dish on the floor.*)

It's a party

(**WOMAN 1** *gets on the phone and exits. There is now nothing in common with* **WOMAN 1**'s *and* **WOMAN 2**'s *and* **3**'s *space. Lights remain the same.*)

I'm a party

what day is it anyway

same clothes for three days

three days same

three for days

three days for same

clothes days

days same three same clothes!

(**WOMAN 2** *joins in. A new level of frenzy and breaking.*)

WOMAN 2. Online kindergarten

WOMAN 3. can't refill my cup

WOMAN 2. 100 sales calls

WOMAN 3. can't ask my mom

WOMAN 2. Six logins for six different websites

WOMAN 3. can't take an hour

WOMAN 2. Homework on top of kids

WOMAN 3. On top of meals

WOMAN 2. On top of cleaning

WOMAN 3. locked myself in a room with a chocolate chip cookie and wine

WOMAN 2 & WOMAN 3. three days wine with a chocolate chip cookie

WOMAN 2. locked myself in a cookie for three days

WOMAN 3. locked myself in wine for three days

WOMAN 2. locked myself in clothes for three days

locked myself in a room for three days

WOMAN 3. *(Correcting her.)* I was locked in for three days

WOMAN 2. *(Correcting her.)* I was cocked in for three days

> *(They laugh maniacally; they break.* **WOMAN 1** *smiles through her disapproval. The sound of breaking dishes slows. This turns into a sad melody.* **WOMAN 1** *nods offstage as the lights fade.)*

Scene Five
Highlight With Accessories

> *(Light rises on* **WOMAN 1**. *She has regrouped. Two stagehands stand behind her.)*

WOMAN 1. First, remove clutter.

> *(Lights fade up slightly on* **WOMAN 2** *and* **WOMAN 3** *as they lower to the floor.)*

You cannot

> *(***WOMAN 2** *and* **WOMAN 3** *get on their hands and knees.)*

WOMAN 2. cannot can't cunt

> *(They grind themselves into the ceramic. Light intensifies on* **WOMAN 1**.*)*

WOMAN 1. decorate around clutter.

WOMAN 3. should to the left should to the right

WOMAN 1. So, take an hour or two, and de-clutter your counter tops.

WOMAN 3. I don't have the time

WOMAN 1. Remove decor items that are out-dated and ready to be replaced.

WOMAN 2. humin droolin' gobs of mess sticky taffy yellow on top of green

WOMAN 3. yellow on top of green

WOMAN 1. You can opt to go for a fresh vase of flowers, hanging lamps, or a photo frame.

WOMAN 2. yellow on top

(**WOMAN 2** *and* **WOMAN 3** *really bloody themselves.*)

WOMAN 2 & WOMAN 3. *(To each other.)* ready to be replaced

WOMAN 1. *(Over, irritated.)* How about a bowl full of brightly colored oranges? Bring the outdoors \ in with a bowl full of...

WOMAN 3. the ring in my ear 'cause I don' wanna hear the din under the sys tim flim flam it's a jam pence and penny spent online buying time tears and trails of yellow on top of green seen under the insanity crisscrossing inanity under the poodles and plaids make me a cowboy with a lasso you know the best times are when you can breathe the range!

(**WOMAN 2** *cowers, checking* **WOMAN 1.**)

WOMAN 1. No matter what you accesso \ rize on your counters, decorate in groups of three to four.

(**WOMAN 2** *and* **WOMAN 3** *try to rise but they are stuck.*)

WOMAN 2 & WOMAN 3. \ rise

WOMAN 1. These accesso \ ries

WOMAN 2 & WOMAN 3. rise

WOMAN 1. will make you feel inspired whenever preparing family meals and also create an artistic kitchen appearance.

(Stagehands pull out paper towels. They begin dropping them on **WOMAN 2** *and* **WOMAN 3**.*)*

WOMAN 2 & WOMAN 3. on top of the best times on top of the best

(**WOMAN 2** *and* **WOMAN 3** *take the paper towels and begin cleaning up the blood. They*

> *wipe their brows with the same paper towels while stagehands and* **WOMAN 1** *watch.)*

WOMAN 2 & WOMAN 3. the best times

in a cookie

locked

> *(Fade to black. Sound of crunching ceramic, then silence. Then the sound of ceramic being swept up.)*

End of Play

pearl apple penguin

Aisling Towl

CHARACTERS

PEARL – Sixty-seven
APPLE – Twenty-eight
SAFFRON – Twenty-five

SETTING

The penguin enclosure at London Zoo.

TIME

Now.

AUTHOR'S NOTES

Quiet penguin noises throughout the play.

In terms of spacing / where the actors should look – the penguins are the audience.

(**PEARL** *is alone on stage, watching the penguins, captivated. Enter* **APPLE** *with a mop and bucket and other cleaning equipment.*)

APPLE. Hi.

Hi.

Uh, sorry. Excuse me.

...Hello.

...HELLO!

(**PEARL** *turns around.*)

Sorry.

PEARL. Oh, no. They're scared now. You've put them on edge.

APPLE. Um, Madam, the penguin enclosure is closing now. Sorry, the whole zoo is closing now so if I could ask you to –

PEARL. What time is it?

APPLE. Uh. Five to seven.

PEARL. I've got five minutes.

APPLE. No, no, sorry, we have to ask everyone to leave so we can clean the enclosure. I need to clean the enclosure.

PEARL. You've scared them with your shouting, look, they're all hiding.

APPLE. Really...?

PEARL. I've never seen them do that before. Are you new here?

APPLE. Yes.

PEARL. What's your name?

APPLE. Apple.

PEARL. Apple?

APPLE. Yes.

PEARL. That's a funny –

APPLE. My parents are musicians.

PEARL. Wonderful. My name's Pearl.

APPLE. Nice to meet you.

PEARL. And you.

APPLE. I really need to ask you to –

PEARL. I know Marcia.

APPLE. Oh. Okay.

PEARL. Marcia and I go way back actually. *Way* back.

APPLE. ...Sorry I don't think I know who Marcia is?

PEARL. She's in charge of amphibians.

(Pause.)

APPLE. I'm from an agency, so.

PEARL. Oh.

APPLE. I really need to clean the penguin enclosure now, if I could ask you to –

PEARL. An *agency*?

APPLE. I really don't want to get –

PEARL. While she cleans, she lets me stay.

APPLE. Who?

PEARL. Marcia.

APPLE. I've been told that –

PEARL. They can't see me from the office anyway. Look. Can they?

> (**APPLE** *turns away from* **PEARL**, *takes a deep breath and speaks quietly to herself.*)

APPLE. I'm breaking with old patterns and moving forward with my life.

PEARL. Sorry?

APPLE. I am important. I am –

> (*She gets out a folded piece of paper from her pocket.*)

I am worthy of love.

PEARL. Mmmm.

> (*Silence.* **APPLE** *puts the piece of paper back in her pocket.*)

APPLE. Okay. You can stay for five minutes. Just while I wash the sides down. Then you really have to –

PEARL. Deal.

> (**APPLE** *starts cleaning.*)

So you don't know Marcia. Do you know Dexter?

APPLE. I don't know.

PEARL. Dexter is a reptilian man, himself. And Marcia takes care of the amphibians. I've been coming here for years, so.

APPLE. Are penguins even classified as amphibians?

(**PEARL** *is visibly horrified.*)

PEARL. Is this your full-time job?

APPLE. Yes.

PEARL. And you hope to be a zoologist?

APPLE. A what?

PEARL. A ZOO-O-LOG-IST?

APPLE. I don't think so.

PEARL. Penguins are an aquatic flightless bird. Birds are not mammals. Live birth is a common trait of mammals but not always a…a…defining trait. The platypus is famous for being a mammal that lays eggs.

(*Pause.*)

Another common of mammals trait is that they have hair. Well, most mammals have hair there are some who do not. Dolphins are the first that come to mind. They have hair as a baby but it quickly falls out. Penguins have none of these. They do not have mammary glands to produce milk for their young. Do penguins have hair? No they do not. Penguins are not mammals.

APPLE. I know they're not mammals.

PEARL. Then we're agreed.

APPLE. So your friend Marcia is the –

PEARL. In charge of amphibians, yes. She usually comes and meets me here. How do you find the job?

APPLE. It's fine. It's cleaning. There's something um, satisfying about cleaning.

PEARL. Oh, I don't think so. It would be a lot more satisfying not to have to do it.

APPLE. What do you do? Or what did you –

PEARL. What did I do?

APPLE. For a living?

PEARL. I'm an artist.

APPLE. Oh. Cool. What's your medium?

PEARL. People.

APPLE. ...great. Well, listen, it was really nice meeting you, um, Pearl, and I hope you have a nice evening, but. I really have to ask politely if you could make your way toward the main exit now.

PEARL. No thank you.

APPLE. Please.

PEARL. I'd really like to stay.

APPLE. I'm going to get in trouble.

PEARL. You won't.

APPLE. It's only my second day.

PEARL. Then they can't expect you to know what you're doing –

APPLE. I don't know if this is about the environment or or if you're part of some kind of group or something that's fine I support that kind of thing but I'm really sorry it's not fair to, to, I'm literally on seven-eighty an hour, I'm going to have to call security in a minute if you don't leave, I really, really don't want to do that, I don't know what they do but I don't want them to kick you out it won't be nice, and I don't want to get in trouble, and you can come back tomorrow we open at nine, you can stay all day and look at the penguins, you just can't stay right now.

PEARL. I won't be able to come back tomorrow.

APPLE. Is this about the environment? Are you part of a group?

(Pause.)

PEARL. I don't think so.

APPLE. Are there other people hiding in other parts of the zoo?

(Pause.)

PEARL. There could be.

APPLE. I just don't see how it's, you'll never get through to the people in charge, they won't even notice, it'll just mean we all have to stay late and security will chuck you out, and I had to check, with myself, before I took this job, whether I could ethically, if it was ethically okay to work in zoos, even cleaning, because it contributes, you know and I did a lot of reading, and I came to the conclusion that because they do conservation work, a lot of environmentalist work, it's –

PEARL. I'm not here about the environment. I'm just waiting for Marcia.

APPLE. Waiting for her?

PEARL. To finish work.

APPLE. Can't you wait for her outside?

PEARL. We always meet here.

APPLE. Either way you're going to have to leave, so you might as well – I really, really don't want to call security –

PEARL. So don't call them.

APPLE. Should I just go and find Marcia? I'll radio Marcia, then you can –

PEARL. No.

APPLE. I'll just radio her, then she can –

PEARL. NO NO NO NO NO NO NO NO –

APPLE. *(Speaking into her radio.)* Apple to Marcia. *(Silence.)* Apple to Marcia. *(Silence.)* Apple to management.

(We hear "Receiving" from the radio.)

Is Marcia on shift?

"Marcia...?...There's no one called Marcia that works here.

Do you need assistance?"

No. Thank you, out.

(Awful silence.)

PEARL. That was an incredibly unkind thing to do.

APPLE. Wow, okay, sorry to burst your bubble, I'm just trying to do my job.

PEARL. Does your job define you?

APPLE. What? I – come on –

PEARL. Have you not your own free will?

APPLE. Not for seven-eighty an hour!

PEARL. You can't put a price on –

APPLE. I DON'T WANT TO LOSE MY JOB.

PEARL. Okay –

APPLE. BUT I DON'T WANT TO CALL SECURITY ON YOU EITHER BECAUSE IT WILL BE HORRIBLE SO PLEASE JUST LEAVE. PLEASE JUST LEAVE, PLEASE LEAVE.

*(**PEARL** carries on watching the penguins. **APPLE** gets out her paper, takes a deep, deep breath.)*

> I give myself permission to do what is right for me. I trust that I am on the right path. I am inspired, and not scared by the world around me. I am –

PEARL. They think I'm one of the penguins. One of them.

APPLE. They don't.

PEARL. I think they do.

APPLE. Are you real?

PEARL. Are you real?

APPLE. No.

PEARL. I'm real.

APPLE. Can other people see you?

> (**PEARL** *does not understand.* **APPLE** *carries on cleaning.*)

PEARL. Marcia and I met at about your age. We worked in a factory that made filing cabinets. On my first day I hated it there and I knew I was going to hate it the whole time I worked there. "Give in to it" – people would say. "Give in to it" and "enjoy it" – variations on that theme. Marcia wore a badge. A little red badge with a hammer and a sickle – a tiny little button. Still – dangerous. We didn't even have to talk. Just looks. Looks can be a thousand words.

And I'd like to tell you we burnt it to the ground, or hollowed it out, filled it up with something better, something good, but of course we didn't, and it's still there. We did shake things up, though, we did cause a stir. And the ripples of that became material, so in a way, yes, in a way, we changed the fabric of reality, portions of it, erased and re-written. You have to imagine it first. You have to dare to imagine it.

We lived together in a commune. On the outskirts. She went to college to do small animal handling. I made art. Marcia had a certain affinity with animals, it was a gift. I've always been so happy for her that she had that – that connection to something else.

(Pause.)

APPLE. Sometimes I think I can read people's minds.

PEARL. Yes, good.

APPLE. Like, I think I can hear them thinking horrible things about me, before they've even – like, we'll be having a normal conversation about food or whatever but in my head I'm like, thinking about how much they hate...my hair? But, to quite an extreme point where it's very much real and I'm sort of convinced that they are actually thinking it and that they want me to know?

PEARL. Your hair?

APPLE. Not my hair specifically, that's just one of the things... I guess it's more often I'm convinced that they know I'm like, fundamentally a terrible person? And I can hear them thinking about it as I'm literally speaking to them about something, like, really mundane.

PEARL. You're a fundamentally terrible person?

APPLE. Oh, I just am. Like, the way I am with my siblings, we're not nice to each other. I can't make relationships work, I think I deliberately seek out bad ones. I think I'm deeply selfish even when I really try hard not to be. I think about things when I'm having sex, like...violence or online clothes shopping. I don't listen to people very well. I consume lots of things I don't need and I want to have kids one day rather than adopt even though –

PEARL. Penguins don't fly, doesn't mean they're mammals.

APPLE. Can you leave now, please?

PEARL. I'm waiting for Marcia.

APPLE. Marcia doesn't exist.

PEARL. Sometimes I shout how I'm feeling into the universe – questions, or words – into the universe and wait for an answer.

APPLE. I just want to clean the enclosure and go home.

PEARL. The answer doesn't always come. But it makes you feel better.

APPLE. It would make me feel better if you –

PEARL. ...CONFUSION

...GRIEF

...ACHING

> *(The penguins make louder noises in response.)*

> *(**APPLE** is unsure but desperate.)*

APPLE. ANGER

...FRUSTRATION

...PAIN

PEARL. ...BURNING

APPLE. ...NUMB

...EMPTY

PEARL. ...MARCIA

APPLE. ...I don't want to say the person's name?

PEARL. ...WHO DO YOU WRITE ALL THOSE LETTERS TO?

APPLE. ...WHY DO YOU MAKE SO MUCH NOISE IN YOUR SLEEP?

PEARL. ...HOW COME YOU'RE SUCH A WONDERFUL DANCER?

APPLE. ...WHY DO YOU HAVE SUCH BEAUTIFUL HANDS?

PEARL. ...WHERE DID YOU GO? OH, WHERE DID YOU GO?

(The penguins make even louder noises.)

APPLE. ...WHY DIDN'T YOU TELL ME YOU WERE MARRIED?

(Enter **SAFFRON.***)*

SAFFRON. Everything alright, Apple?

APPLE. Saffron!

PEARL. Marcia!

SAFFRON. Pearl! Sorry I'm late.

APPLE. Sorry, sorry, I've done the, I was just asking her to –

SAFFRON. Pearl, do you want to wait for me at the gate? I'll be there in two minutes.

PEARL. Perfect, I've brought jam tarts.

(She leaves, patting **APPLE** *on the shoulder.)*

APPLE. She thinks you're Marcia?

SAFFRON. We take turns.

APPLE. ...

SAFFRON. All of us in the office. You say you're Marcia, you're Marcia, she leaves. We take turns walking her to the bus stop.

APPLE. Every day?

SAFFRON. Most days.

APPLE. Oh.

SAFFRON. She's great, isn't she?

APPLE. Who is Marcia?

SAFFRON. No idea. Her ex? I don't know.

APPLE. Did she used to work here?

SAFFRON. I never met her if she did. You need to make sure you use the blue liquid on the sides or it goes funny, did you not use the blue liquid?

APPLE. Oh, I used the pink. Sorry.

SAFFRON. I'm worried about the penguins, you know. They're at risk. You don't think to worry about them as a species because whenever you see them on TV there's just so many of them, you know? Just getting on with things. But they are, they're struggling. I feel bad for them.

The End

Grieved.

Jahquale Mazyck

CHARACTERS

MAN
WOMAN

(*A **BLACK WOMAN** and a **BLACK MAN** sit next to each other. A casket is not there physically but it is there.*)

MAN. So sad.

WOMAN. Mhm.

MAN. He was young.

WOMAN. Yeah, young.

MAN. Younger than me.

WOMAN. Yeah.

MAN. Younger than us.

WOMAN. Young.

MAN. Half of us couldn't even make a whole of him. That's how young he is.

That's how young he *was*. Taken so young. Too young to be taken.

WOMAN. Mhm.

MAN. I feel like he was my son.

WOMAN. He *was*.

MAN. What?

WOMAN. *Was* your son. *Is* your son. You didn't know him for long. But –

Yeah.

Your son. *Young*.

MAN. Oh.

Wow. My own son. Taken from me. So young.

WOMAN. Young Son.

MAN. He was good. Honest. Honest as they come. Tall and strong. He would've been a great –

WOMAN. You remembering wrong.

MAN. No. He was tall.

WOMAN. Young Son was shorter than me.

MAN. Oh.

WOMAN. Usedta steal dollars from the beggars. Buy sodas with 'em. Usedta take dollars and drink with the dollars he took.

MAN. Well… He was honest to me.

WOMAN. Mhm.

MAN. A good Son.

WOMAN. …

MAN. And His stealing still don't make it right. Don't make their wrong right.

And it don't make him not right. Him stealing don't make him vulnerable to –

He ain't deserve it – how they gave it to him. He ain't deserve it. No one does.

He was good enough. Good enough to live.

My Son. Young Son.

WOMAN. Young Son.

MAN. He was a child. Only a child.

WOMAN. Mhm.

MAN. And Young.

WOMAN. Mhmm.

MAN. …

WOMAN. ...

MAN. Can you sing that song? You know the one that goes like –

WOMAN. Already sung it.

MAN. But –

WOMAN. Last week, at Young Man funeral. Can't sing the same song twice. Loses its meaning when it's repeated. It's like wearing your first wedding dress to the second wedding. Don't feel special no more. Don't feel right. Song feels used after you already sang it to someone. After they take that song it ain't yours no more.

MAN. Right.

How about that other –?

WOMAN. Sang it for Older Man's funeral. Yesterday. He loved that song, so I gave it to him as a parting gift.

MAN. Oh. Ain't there's one that –

WOMAN. Sang it for my own Son. On Sunday. And Monday. Tuesday too. That song old tired. Got a hoarseness to it. Got a tired so strong some of the words don't even come out. The ones that do end up clawing on my throat on the way.

MAN. How about what you sang for little girl's funeral?

WOMAN. We don't sing for little girls.

MAN. Right.

WOMAN. I'm afraid I'm all sung out. I got some prayers left though. Good ones.

MAN. Sure.

WOMAN. Okay.

MAN. ...

WOMAN. I'll say 'em tonight. I'm a little tired right now.

MAN. Aren't we all?

I usedta pray for him. Pray that he get home safe. Pray harm don't find him and latch on. Now I pray that he make it safe to heaven. That there ain't no tolls on the way. I pray God look past the dollars he been taken and see what's been taken from him. I pray he find peace. Seems like the hardest thing to buy these days.

WOMAN. Mhm.

MAN. You know what else?

I pray for vengeance some nights. That's when I pray the hardest. I let the knees bruise on those prayers. I pray for fire and pain. A plague upon their houses. I pray God take their boys just like they took mine. I plead for agony to greet them like it did me. I be asking for justice but –

I ain't too sure it's coming.

WOMAN. ...

Well good luck with that.

MAN. Been thinking about doing it myself.

WOMAN. Mhm.

MAN. Taking a gun. Taking the pain. And bringing it to them.

WOMAN. Big Man.

MAN. I could do it.

Could do it. *Might*.

I'd bring it to 'em. Like they brought it to us.

Like they keep bringing.

Lay it at their door. Lay it down.

Let it find them. Like they found us.

Imma wait. Like they wait.

One wrong move. One wrong word.

Boom.

End it there. Like they end us – anywhere.

Anywhere. I could do it. Might do it.

WOMAN. *Might.*

MAN. Can do it.

WOMAN. – *Can.*

MAN. You don't / think.

WOMAN. I don't believe you.

MAN. I would.

WOMAN. Would.

MAN. For my Son. Young Son.

WOMAN. Mhmm.

MAN. You don't think I could.

WOMAN. I don't think you *will*.

MAN. I could. Can. Maybe. You don't know. I might. I would bring it to 'em. Bring it down like a hammer on their heads. I wouldn't even blink. Wouldn't even say sorry. I would just watch. Record. Send. Share. Comment – Not comment. Condemn. "Why was he out so late?" "Why he look so suspicious?" "Should've put his hands up." "Should've kept his hands in his pockets" "Should've left." "Should've gone home" "Shouldn't have been home." "Shouldn't have left the door unlocked." "What's he hiding?" "What's he showing?" Boom.

Boom.

Boom.

WOMAN. I don't think you will.

MAN. You don't think I can.

WOMAN. Nah.

MAN. Why?

WOMAN. 'Cause you said this before.

MAN. No I –

WOMAN. So many / times.

MAN. No I / didn't.

WOMAN. So many / ways.

MAN. I've never felt like *this*.

WOMAN. So many / funerals.

MAN. Rage like this.

WOMAN. It goes.

MAN. No.

WOMAN. It passes.

MAN. …

WOMAN. You have other Sons. You *had* other Sons.

MAN. Not like him. Young Son.

WOMAN. They never get old enough. They never become old enough.

MAN. But he was –

WOMAN. Good.

MAN. He was –

WOMAN. Good enough.

MAN. I can do it. I can bring it to them. Like they brought it to him.

WOMAN. You said it before. With just as much rage. Just as much anger. And then it fades. Not as much conviction. And then it happens. And then we sit. And then you ask me to sing. And I say I have no more songs. I say I am tired. And you say that it's time. To bring it to them. But you don't. Because the next one has to be planned. The next Young Son has to be buried and mourned for. So we move. And we sit. And we move. And we sit. Sometimes we march. Sometimes we chant. Sometimes we sing. Only for the Young Sons. Never for the little girls. I used to get angry at that. Usedta see unfairness in that.

MAN. So why don't *you* get mad? Why don't *you* change it?

WOMAN. Mad don't do much for me these days. Besides people like your *mad* better than mine.

MAN. That's 'cause I ain't scared to fight. I ain't scared to bring it to them.

WOMAN. Mhm.

MAN. I will fight to my last fucking breath.

Even when I can't breathe. I fight.

And I'll bring my no-more-breath-fight to them. Just like they bring it to me.

WOMAN. Okay, Big Man.

MAN. And you ought to do the same. You outta sing even if you tired. You outta sing for Young Son even if you sung the song before. It's lazy if you don't. *Dangerous.*

WOMAN. Mhm.

MAN. Ain't you scared of that? Being lazy? Too lazy to fight. Too lazy to not move. Too lazy to live. Livin' lazy ain't no life at all.

WOMAN. This isn't much of a life, is it?

MAN. No. But we can change it.

WOMAN. Go change it then.

MAN. You think I can't. You think I won't?

WOMAN. Don't matter what I think. None of my thoughts matter much these days. I say go do it 'cause it's what you want to do. Don't do it to prove a point. Don't gotta prove nothing to me. I say do it 'cause you say you gonna do it. Announce it. Shout it. Plan it. Visualize. Analyze it. Deconstruct it. Write it. Dance it. Sing it. Chant it. Amplify it. Do what you gotta do. But don't do it 'cause someone say you can't. Don't do it for me. 'Cause I don't care enough to care about what you do – or what you don't do.

MAN. Fine.

*(**MAN** stands. Ready to exit. He halts.)*

You gon' come with me?

WOMAN. My legs tired.

MAN. You gon' wait for me?

WOMAN. Can't go nowhere. Can't do nothing but wait.

MAN. You gonna wait by yourself?

WOMAN. Who else Imma wait with? Young Son?

MAN. Where your children?

WOMAN. Same place they've *been* – on my mind. In my heart. In your prayers.

(Heaven.)

MAN. You sing for them?

WOMAN. For the Young Sons. The little girls ain't get no song though.

MAN. …

WOMAN. It's hard.

Hard to come up with something for them. Even harder to get people to listen and sing along.

MAN. I'll sing with you.

WOMAN. Huh.

MAN. I would.

WOMAN. Mhm.

Can't sing now anyway. Moment's gone. A song out of moment ain't a song. It's just noise. I ain't in the business of making noise. Noise don't do much for me these days.

Noise never did much for me.

Just made things hard.

MAN. ...

> (**MAN** *comes back in and sit nexts to* **WOMAN**. **MAN** *starts to hum a tune.* **WOMAN** *is disgusted by its out of tune-ness.)*

WOMAN. What the hell is that?

MAN. My song for you. For your girl who passed.

WOMAN. Which one?

MAN. ...

The uh...

Um...

Uh...

dark skin.

WOMAN. huh.

MAN. Brown eyes.

WOMAN. Mhm.

MAN. Medium height. You know which one I'm talking 'bout.

Sweet Thing.

WOMAN. *Sweet Thing.*

MAN. Yeah. Never hurt a fly. No disrespect. Sat straight. Sat quiet. Nice girl.

Sweet Thing.

WOMAN. Sweet Thing.

MAN. Always smiled, when I smiled. Always nodded when I nodded. Poor thing.

Sweet Thing.

WOMAN. Sweet Thing.

MAN. Yeah. Imma sing for her.

> (**MAN** *sings. It's actually quite beautiful.* **WOMAN** *cries.*)

I'm sorry. Wound too raw?

WOMAN. Wound ain't even a wound yet.

Sweet Thing still here. She still living. That's why I'm crying. She don't know death yet.

MAN. Hey maybe she won't ever know it like we know it.

WOMAN. *Please.*

It's funny tho. Funny how you know Sweet Thing. Funny that you don't know her at all. Most People *don't* know her. People don't see her. They get a glimpse but never the full thing. She so bright. Got a fire too.

Ain't sweet like y'all think. Ain't sweet at all. She angry. But that good angry. An Angry that got purpose – direction. A mad that make you wanna do something. That's why I'm crying.

MAN. Well give that song to her next time you see her. Maybe she could use it.

Wish I could've gave Young Son one. Seem like a crime to only sing when they die.

WOMAN. Mhm.

MAN. *Young Son.*

WOMAN. *Sweet Thing.*

MAN. Hey.

Lemme walk you home. Sing to you on the way. Give you a new song. Just for you to carry.

WOMAN. Cute.

But I ain't walking home. I gotta go to Lil Boy's memorial service after this.

MAN. Oh right.

Who Son that is?

WOMAN. *(Breathes.)* Ours.

MAN. Oh right.

You gonna be singing?

WOMAN. Nah. Not today. Too tired.

MAN. I feel you.

I'd sing but –

WOMAN. You ain't gotta.

MAN. I would.

WOMAN. Don't need to.

MAN. I can.

WOMAN. Mhm.

MAN. I could.

WOMAN. *Could.*

MAN. You don't think I can?

WOMAN. What we think don't matter much these days.

MAN. Well, I might.

WOMAN. *Might.*

MAN. Yeah. If I wasn't so –

WOMAN. Right.

MAN. It's just hard to –

WOMAN. Right.

MAN. It's all so...you know.

WOMAN. ... *(Nods.)*

MAN. It's *Sad*.

WOMAN. huh.

MAN. So sad.

WOMAN. Mhm.

MAN. ...sad.

WOMAN. ...

MAN. ...

(They sit in silence. And sit. And sit.)

End Scene

Dogs of Society

Julia Grogan

CHARACTERS

JOY – mid-late twenties, black, smart
LYDIA – mid-twenties, bites her nails
NICK – late-twenties, outrageously attractive, sensitive
TOM – thirties, driven, a little more sunken
PRODUCER – is a voice. A man's voice. We hate him.

AUTHOR'S NOTES

Any <u>dialogue</u> in italics is script from the reality TV show.

Not all punctuation is grammatical.

(*JOY is alone, harsh light smacking her right in the face. She's pouring her heart out to anyone that'll listen. This is a performance of a goddamn lifetime.*)

JOY. *I fucking let my guard down with you. No Nick. Let me – let me feel. Your ex? Are you actually fucking kidding me? I am so embarrassed. How could you? How could you do this to me? I turned my back on my friends for you – I – I am so bewildered and lost and –*

(*The voice of a* **PRODUCER** *cuts through.*)

PRODUCER. Sorry Joy. Can we go back to... I am so bewildered and lost?

(*JOY blinks into the light.*)

JOY. Yeah. No problem.

PRODUCER. And less tears, we're sponsored by Maybelline not Tampax.

JOY. Yeah. Sure. Sorry.

(*She sniffs. Runs her fingers under her eyes.*)

OK?

(*Beat.*)

I am so bewildered and lost and –

PRODUCER. Sorry – fly on the lens. Bewildered and lost in three...two...one...

JOY. *I feel so bewildered and lost and –*

There's a woman. She grew up with small tits so developed a mean, bold personality while she waited for them to grow. She sucked dick. A lot during high school. The word whore was chucked about. She still feels it stuck to the back of her teeth. She's never had to have a job. She's privileged. But she masks it by sending hand-me-downs to Calais. She doesn't make eye contact with homeless people. She's contemplated a lip job but spent the money on her tits instead. This made her happy. The people were happy. In fact they talk to her tits now. Not her face. Just her tits. It's –

PRODUCER. Perfect. Okay –

> (**JOY** *is gone.* **NICK** *has taken her place in the light.*)

NICK. There's a man –

PRODUCER. We're going to get a shot of him coming out the sea. Yeah. Nick can you flick your nips? We need them hard for the over head. Nice. Okay.

NICK. There's a man and he's fucking freezing. Emotionally and physically. He's enjoying the press of pebbles on his feet. He digs his weight down further to the back of his heel and feels a broken shell cut into his skin. He's attractive. Ridiculously so. The kind you wouldn't see associated with cancer or terror attacks. He swallows Viagra to rouse his floppy cock and then he fucks women firmly. Relentlessly. By the end of the day his dick is *so* tired. Because it is *so* wanted. Everyone wants it. He transcends human form. His jaw could cut through a slab of raw meat. He's deadly. He's –

PRODUCER. Onto the next take. Thank you.

> (**LYDIA** *has taken* **NICK**'s *place.*)

LYDIA. *I just need to get out the city I think. I think that's what I need. Just take a break. Just get out of the city. Just.*

There's a woman and she's talking to another woman.

JOY. *Babe I haven't seen you for like a week? How's everything with the fashion campaign?*

LYDIA. She's hardly met this woman. But this woman is her best friend. There's a woman and she's messy. She masturbates to the Headspace App and if it's Harry Styles reading a bed time story she uses a G spot vibrator on her arse hole. Around. Never in. She's dirty. But she wears perfume. She flips her knickers inside out when she can't wash them. She's tired. Crusty. She doesn't sleep. There's a woman and she sips on fifteen pound drinks that are mostly ice. She's slim and sleek. She's terrified of dying without a Wikipedia page so she spent a year signing up to reality TV shows. Sometimes she feels alone in the world, sometimes so alone she –

PRODUCER. Lyd you've got coke round your nose.

LYDIA. Fuck. Sorry.

PRODUCER. Other nostril.

LYDIA. Sorry it's icing sugar. I had a donut for lunch –

PRODUCER. Yeah and I had Katy Perry's vag. Next scene.

(**TOM** *has replaced* **LYDIA**.)

TOM. *I've decided this year we're going big with the company. Just like huge. I want the app to just explode. Do you feel me? Like I want take off. I want to take the fuck off.*

There's a man. And he's got grand plans. Grand plans that will be done by this man. He's built an app with his bare hands. The app is h-app-ening. He's a hunter gatherer of data and communication. He IS the future. He was podgy at primary school but now it's war weight. He licks his lips because he knows this app is just going to change things. For the better. And he's sitting on it. Patiently like a throne. Waiting to strike.

There's a man and –

PRODUCER. There's a hash tag circulating round about you.

(*Beat.*)

TOM. What?

PRODUCER. We're suspending you from Season Nine while we review. Sorry Tom. I've got Twitter breathing down my neck, my hands are tied.

(*There's space. Then –.*)

(**TOM**'s *phone rings. He picks it up. Game face.*)

TOM. Hi hun. Yeah everything's good. We're all good.

Quirky Café

*(**JOY** and **LYDIA** are smiling at each other in a café. They are <u>glowing</u>.)*

JOY. *Oh my God. Are you hanging?*

LYDIA. *I've like never been this hungover. Literally.*

*(**JOY** laughs and sips on a matcha latte.)*

Such a good night though.

JOY. *Yeah. Such a good night.*

LYDIA. *I can't cope with you and Nick. Are you back together?*

JOY. *Yeah. Course. I'm just taking it slow.*

LYDIA. *I think you just need to drop your guard babe and let him in. Like, ignore all the toxicity of last year.*

JOY. *I know. I know I should I just…*

(She stiffens, looks into her drink, striking a perfect angle with her jaw.)

LYDIA. *Oh my God babe.*

JOY. *Sorry, I'm getting upset.*

LYDIA. *Oh my God babe don't get upset.*

*(**LYDIA** reaches out a hand and stiffly cups **JOY**'s elbow.)*

Literally. Like.

JOY. *I know. It's just. Hard.*

LYDIA. *Well. Focus on the present. Things with him are going <u>super</u> well now. I mean, I heard it last night.*

*(She raises her eyebrow. **JOY** giggles shyly into her latte, deflects –.)*

JOY. *How's everything with you though babe? You look so empowered lately.*

LYDIA. *Thanks babe. Yeah. I am actually feeling like so empowered. Like I wake up and the first person I think about is me. Number one. And it's really freeing. Like so empowering.*

JOY. *I'm so happy for you.*

PRODUCER. Okay cut. Back in a two.

> (*The women drop their smiles.* **LYDIA** *looks out the window passively.* **JOY** *takes out an eyebrow pencil and starts shading her brows.*)

LYDIA. Weather's nice.

JOY. It's grey.

LYDIA. I like it grey. Everyone looks like they belong in an art gallery. It's cool.

JOY. It's depressing.

> (*Beat.*)

LYDIA. For someone called Joy you're very cynical.

JOY. I'm not called Joy.

LYDIA. – ?

JOY. My name's Johari.

LYDIA. Why do they call you Joy?

> (**JOY** *shrugs.*)

JOY. Easier.

> (**LYDIA** *nods.*)

LYDIA. I used to watch you in the show. You look amazing on camera. Have you ever watched yourself?

JOY. Of course.

LYDIA. There was an episode of you. I think it was. Season Two Episode Three. You'd just been told you could never have children or something. You were wearing this like chiffon pink coat. It was amazing.

JOY. Yeah. I remember.

LYDIA. Did you always want to be on TV?

    (**JOY** *looks up from her make up.*)

JOY. No. I wanted to be a lawyer.

LYDIA. That's amazing. Did you study?

JOY. Yes.

LYDIA. Where did you study?

    (**JOY** *puts her make up down and sits back.*)

JOY. Cambridge.

LYDIA. Fuck. Wow. So you're really smart. And pretty.

Why did you drop out –

JOY. Where's Nina? My hair needs doing.

LYDIA. She's taking a call.

You have beautiful hair. It's so thick and glossy. My hair looks like Gandalf's pubes. I blow dry it upside down and it still lies flat.

    (**JOY** *runs her hand through her hair –.*)

JOY. I've never thought much of my hair –

    (*The flick knocks her make up bag on the floor.*)

Fuck.

LYDIA. Don't worry.

>(*An orange tub of pills falls on the floor by* **LYDIA**'s *feet.*)

Oh. You've.

>(**LYDIA** *picks up the pills, studying the tub.* **JOY** *snatches them off her.*)

PRODUCER. *(Laboured.)* Guys we're going to move location to the Brasserie. Someone's just been stabbed outside and the sirens are pissing me off. Just ignore his body and Shona will walk you over it. Watch your heels.

He's decided to bleed.

Everywhere.

Product Placement

> (**LYDIA** *is facing* **NICK** *and* **JOY**. *The pair are arm in arm,* **NICK** *cradling a bottle of Moët like a newborn.*)

LYDIA. *So? What is it?*

> (*Beat.*)

JOY. *We're getting married!*

LYDIA. *You're getting married?*

> (**LYDIA** *looks at* **NICK**, *holds it for two seconds.*)

That's amazing.

> (**NICK** *shifts mechanically.*)

NICK. *We can't wait –*

JOY. *And...*

> (*She looks at* **NICK** *for permission...he grants it.*)

I want you to be my maid of honour.

LYDIA. *You don't mean that.*

JOY. *Seriously. There's no one else I'd rather have babe. Trust. You'll be amazing. So is it a yes?*

LYDIA. *Course it is babe. I'm thrilled.*

> (*They awkwardly hold their faces in the same position. For three, two, one...*)

PRODUCER. Adverts.

> (*Faces drop.*)

NICK. Did I get the label in?

(He spins a bottle of Moët round a bit more.)

JOY. Yeah I think so.

New Year's Party

(**LYDIA** *is rolling a cigarette.* **NICK** *is eating a sandwich.*)

LYDIA. So you're not sexually attracted to me.

NICK. Umm. Sorry. Is that awkward?

LYDIA. No. No. That's honest.

(*Beat.*)

Is it my nose?

NICK. No. It's not your nose.

LYDIA. But you've noticed it?

NICK. What?

LYDIA. My nose. You've noticed it.

NICK. Well I've noticed you've got a nose. Like everyone. Everyone has a nose.

LYDIA. Apart from Voldemort.

NICK. Yeah. Apart from him.

(*She rolls her cig between her fingers.*)

LYDIA. Do you love Joy?

NICK. You ask a lot of questions.

LYDIA. I'm new. I'm allowed to ask questions.

NICK. You've been on the show for six months now. That's not new.

LYDIA. Oh. Right.

(*Beat.*)

Will they replace me soon?

NICK. Depends.

> *(He watches* **LYDIA**, *her hand nervously twitching.)*

In answer to your question. Yes. I do love Joy. We've been on and off since Ep One.

LYDIA. I didn't mean in the show.

> *(***NICK** *goes back to eating his sandwich.)*

NICK. In that case, I've been in love with the same man since I was nine.

LYDIA. Does he mind? You know. That you're in love with Joy?

NICK. He's dead.

LYDIA. Oh. Right.

NICK. He was hit by a Cross Town donut van. The icing sugar exploded everywhere like a bomb. Kids made snow angels in the dust for weeks after.

LYDIA. Fuck. I'm sorry. I bet that hurt.

> *(Beat.)*

PRODUCER. Okay guys. Are we good?

NICK. Yep.

LYDIA. All good.

PRODUCER. Quiet on set.

> *(***LYDIA** *and* **NICK** *resume position.)*

NICK. *Because the thing is, I know I'm marrying Joy. But I've. Look, since you arrived here I haven't been able to stop looking at you.*

> *(***LYDIA** *blushes, cradling a red wine in her sweaty hand.)*

And. I sort of. Really want to kiss you.

> *(He half smiles.)*

> *(She shoots him a look of pure innocence – lust – vulnerability – sex demon.)*

LYDIA. *Why don't you then?*

> *(They start kissing. With tongues. It's gross.)*

Nondescript Café / Bar

LYDIA. I was told to.

JOY. Nice.

LYDIA. Come on, please. I had to.

JOY. We're not allowed to talk about this until the camera's rolling. It's in the contract.

LYDIA. Please.

JOY. I'm not arguing with you over a man. I'm far too fucking smart for that.

LYDIA. Are you still getting married?

JOY. What is that smell?

LYDIA. Can you look at me Joy? Please?

JOY. Lydia you stink.

LYDIA. Sorry. My. I'll sort it. I'll sort all of this.

JOY. You smell like a dead carcass.

Ibiza Weekender

(The group are lingering awaiting instruction. **TOM** *enters, he looks empty, completely in his own head. The others are background noise.)*

NICK. Tom!

JOY. Fuck –

LYDIA. Hey Tom.

TOM. Not guilty.

NICK. Nice. You must be happy?

TOM. Sorry?

NICK. Happy? You must be glad you're back.

TOM. Oh. Yeah. Yeah. I'm happy.

JOY. We've missed you.

LYDIA. I'm Lydia.

TOM. My wife left me.

JOY. Fuck.

NICK. Great news about the app though right?

TOM. She's taken my kid. Too.

LYDIA. Hi I'm Lydia.

NICK. The launch. That's massive.

TOM. Yeah. Really exciting. I'm on my own now.

PRODUCER. Right. Big man slap. High energy. Let's go.

(Beat.)

*(***NICK*** gives* **TOM** *a massive man slap on the back.)*

NICK. *(Surprised.)* Mate!

JOY. *(Surprised.)* Tom's back.

NICK. Mate, how was Ibiza?

    (Beat.)

TOM. Fucking awesome boyo!!!!

Hashtag

(**NICK** *and* **TOM** *are in the space, staring out. Neither is saying anything.*)

NICK. So did you do it?

TOM. What?

NICK. Pat that girl on the fanny.

TOM. Do I look like I did?

NICK. Well.

TOM. What?

NICK. You're a man. Of course you look like you did.

TOM. I didn't pat anyone on the fanny.

(*Beat.*)

Sometimes I wish I'd applied to the jungle. Don't you? At least then there's the possibility of being mauled to death by a tiger.

NICK. Yeah.

(*Beat.*)

TOM. How are things with Joy?

NICK. I haven't watched the last episode yet.

TOM. You get punched in the face in the next one.

NICK. Nice.

Bar

JOY. So we're moving in together.

TOM. Yes mate. That's amazing.

LYDIA. Is this real?

NICK. Sorry?

LYDIA. What –

PRODUCER. Are we good on set?

JOY. Lydia?

LYDIA. Sorry. My head. Is.

JOY. Are you okay? You look...

LYDIA. I feel like I'm turning into an animal.

NICK. What?

PRODUCER. Are we good?

    (**LYDIA** *sniffs sharply in.*)

LYDIA. Sorry. All good.

PRODUCER. Okay action.

Tom can I grab you for a sec. Thanks for taking the wrap on that fanny pat at the Christmas party. I'm such a cunt after a tequila. I'm getting you a deal with Sensodyne to keep you smiling.

TOM. What?

PRODUCER. That's okay. It's a three mil deal. You can use it for the launch. The launch into space.

Another Nondescript Café / Bar

JOY. I've decided to forgive you.

LYDIA. Do you maybe want to get a drink tonight?

JOY. I can't drink.

LYDIA. –?

JOY. My hair falls out. Particularly in times of stress. So I don't socialise.

LYDIA. That's very sad.

JOY. Thank you –

LYDIA. I love your hair.

JOY. I think you should stop taking cocaine.

LYDIA. I don't take cocaine.

JOY. Right.

LYDIA. Okay I do but just a little bump in the morning. I don't sleep so I.

JOY. You should have a bath. With lavender.

LYDIA. I had a shower this morning.

JOY. I don't mean because you smell. I mean to relax you.

(Beat.)

LYDIA. I always wanted to be seen. I don't think there's anything worse than not being seen.

(Beat.)

Are we on camera?

JOY. I don't even know anymore.

Cry

*(**LYDIA** is standing in the space. She looks empty.)*

PRODUCER. Okay and Joy has thrown a massive gin and tonic in the your face. It's seeping down your neck, your back all the way down into your crack okay? It's fucking freezing.

Home

JOY. There's a woman. She's walking down the road with a broken heel. She can't flag down a taxi because she has no money. Because she spent it all on her tits and her wigs and her teeth and her gins.

Cry

PRODUCER. *(Shouting.)* CRY. CRY. Cry cry cry cry cry cry cry.

CRY.

LYDIA. I can't.

PRODUCER. Get out.

Home

(Evening.)

JOY. There's a woman and she's fixed on every step of her heels against the wet, her wig damp in her hand. Like a dead Black Lab. She turns the corner. She's walking home to her mum's. She's lonely. No one wants to fuck her. She will make pasta bake for her mum who will then hold her close for the night. The woman thinks of the time she was a lawyer. Before her mother needed care. The woman stands with her heels on the edge of the pavement.

NICK. There's a man and he's cupping pills. There's a pink one and a blue one and a green one. He's listening to the sound of the rain outside. He's staring at a photo of his love on the wall. They'd gone to New York before the accident. He clenches his jaw. It is ridiculously defined. It really could cut through raw meat.

LYDIA. There's a woman and she's in the bath. She's lit fourteen candles. It smells like a gang bang of lavender and Christmas. Her phone is pinging. She's reached 1.2 million followers. For every ping she pops a bubble. She really is very famous now. She thinks of all the places she can visit and get free things. She thinks she might go to Whistles and try on a dress. She thinks –

JOY. I could just get a bus round the corner to my mum's. That would make it quicker. Because mum's always waiting. I'm always on time with dinner. I should just get a bus.

TOM. There's a man and his heating's gone off. He's scrolling and scrolling and scrolling through friends doing better than him. His daughter's fairy wings are hanging on the back of the door. Everyone really is doing better than him. There's a man –

LYDIA. And there's a woman –

JOY. Tapping her shoes on the pavement.

NICK. Holding colourful pills in his hand –

TOM. And he opens the window and hears a bus sail past.

NICK. There's a man and he swallows

TOM. He jumps

JOY. She steps

LYDIA. She sinks.

Party of a Lifetime

PRODUCER. Right everyone. So big smiles. Party party party. Can we have Nick's hand on Lydia's thigh. Slightly higher, higher, higher. There. Can we have bitchy eyes from Joy and maybe hair flick. Just let us see that gorgeous hair all the way down your back. Lovely lovely. And Tom – God it's almost like you've done this before isn't it.

Okay and we're rolling in three. Two. One.

(The cast raise their glasses and laugh.)

(Blackout.)

All Things Considered, It Was Probably the Most Productive Meeting the Escondido Unified School District PTA Ever Had

A Zoom Play

A.J. Ditty

ALL THINGS CONSIDERED, IT WAS PROBABLY THE MOST PRODUCTIVE MEETING THE ESCONDIDO UNIFIED SCHOOL DISTRICT PTA EVER HAD was originally presented as part of *Virtual Rule of 7x7* through The Tank's *CyberTank* on July 2-3, 2020 over Zoom. The performance was produced by Brett Epstein, and directed by Ivey Lowe. The cast was as follows:

PATRICIA DONOVAN . . . . Bryn Carter
TED LIPMAN . . . . Max Reinhardsen
ANITA WARNER . . . . Alesandra Nahodil

CHARACTERS

PATRICIA DONOVAN – (early 30s-late 40s) Principal of Escondido High School, hasn't left the house in weeks, a woman on the verge of a nervous breakdown.

TED LIPMAN – (late 20s-late 40s) Pre-Calculus teacher of Escondido High School who's always wanted to be the Calculus teacher, lost the kids in the divorce, desperate for a real human connection.

ANITA WARNER – (late 20s-late 40s) Head of the Activities Committee for Escondido High School, works out her feelings through intense amounts of exercise, one of the most positive people you'll ever meet.

SETTING

Various homes/condos/apartments in Escondido, CA.

TIME

July 2020.

Right at the point in the pandemic when people started to realize that this might be forever.

A NOTE ON CASTING

Escondido, CA is a diverse town and the members of the Escondido Unified School District PTA should reflect that diversity. No all-white casts. Period.

I know this seems like a no-brainer, but you would be SURPRISED.

Coming out of my cage /
And I've been doin' REAL BAD.

– Dominic Russo
A trusted friend
When asked to describe
How quarantine was going.

The Scene

*(An empty Zoom room. **PATRICIA** clicks on, fiddles with a few things.)*

PATRICIA. Good morning parents and teachers.

Good-morn-ing pa-rents and teach-ers.

(Realizing.)

Good morning...parent and teacher.

(She takes a deep breath, then reaches for a glass of wine just off-camera. She finishes the entire glass and lets out a low growl.)

I'm fine, how are you?

I'm fine, how are you?

I'm fine, how are you?

(She gets a notification.)

Fucking hell, Ted, the meeting's at ten not nine-fifty-eight.

*(She lets **TED** in, plasters on a smile. He begins talking animatedly.)*

Ted. You have to unmute yourself. Ted, you HAVE to unmute yourself. TED.

(He stops, realizes, clicks the unmute button.)

TED. Can you hear me?

PATRICIA. I can now! Hahahaha.

TED. Hahaha, yeah, sorry, technology, you know!

PATRICIA. You're early!

TED. Well, ya know, I was just sitting in front of my computer for the past thirty minutes waiting for this thing to start and I figured why not just jump in! No risk, no reward!

How're ya doing?

How're the kids?

PATRICIA. They're um.

How're YOU, Ted?

TED. Well, things have been pretty hard since the divorce.

Gale took the kids so my only real interaction every day is with seventh graders over Zoom and most of that is spent trying to stop them from spamming the chat with a photoshopped picture of me and a horse.

Do you know how to make them stop doing that? I don't want to go into too much detail but the picture's PRETTY graphic, so –

PATRICIA. Oop, hang on, looks like...yup, Anita's here!

TED. Right, but if you know how to get them to stop or any tricks on getting them to, ya know, respect me –

> (**ANITA** *logs in. She drinks out of a sports bottle. She is thriving.*)

ANITA. Good morning, everyone! How're we all feeling today?

PATRICIA. Fine, Anita, how're –

ANITA. Sorry, I'm a bit sweaty, just got back from my morning five, the morning five miles, you know. I wasn't running for a while because of the whole mask thing but then there's this new study from China, have you all read about this, this new study from China, where the virus can only really be spread INDOORS, I'll post it in the chat, but anyway it felt so refreshing to just hit the TRAIL again you know, reconnect with NATURE because we're all just animals after all we need the SUN and the AIR and the EARTH beneath our feet. You all keeping fit?

TED. This morning I found a Cheeto in my couch and then I ate that Cheeto.

PATRICIA. Okay, let's get started. Ted, would you read the minutes from last week's meeting?

TED. Sure, hang on, um.

AH, here we go: "Minutes from the 6/25 Meeting of the Escondido Unified School District Parent Teacher Association. Patricia Donovan welcomed everyone over Zoom. Many attendants could not figure out the mute feature because 'the button isn't where the button should be.'"

PATRICIA. We can skip ahead, Ted.

TED. Oh, sure, right. "Proposal brought to the floor by Gene Rudinsky: This PTA is a colossal waste of everyone's time and should be dissolved until the schools reopen.

Results: Yea-Twenty, Nay-Three.

The meeting then ended abruptly when the twenty yeas all dramatically tried to leave the room at the same time but Mr. Rudinsky did not know how to leave the meeting on his own and had to ask Principal Patricia Donovan to do it for him to which she responded 'Go fuck yourself, Gene' to which Gene responded 'No, you go fuck YOURself, Patricia' which was followed by the kind of silence that follows an earthquake when the world is waiting to breathe again and then –"

PATRICIA. Okay, yes, we all remember the conversation, Ted, thank you. All those in favor of ratifying the minutes say Yea.

ANITA.   **TED.**
Yea.   Yea.

PATRICIA. And yea, the yeas have it. Oh and Ted, you know how much we all love your creativity but, for today's minutes, maybe fewer metaphors and more just basic bullet points, okay?

TED. Sorry, I just started taking this online creative writing class and the instructor said that any writing can be creative writing if you're CREATIVE enough. I will take regular minutes.

PATRICIA. Wonderful. Attendance: Principal Patricia Donovan, President of the PTA, Present.

ANITA. Anita Warner, Head of the Fundraising Committee and proud parent of Brett and Jason Warner, Present.

TED. Ted Lipman, Secretary and Pre-Calculus Teacher, Escondido High School, Present.

PATRICIA. Fantastic. Let's check in with our various...our one committee.

ANITA. Oh, that's me! Right, so, to celebrate the end of the school year, we were thinking about having a little Zoom party for all the classes. We're talking music, we're talking dancing, all from our separate homes. We tried a similar thing last week for Brett's birthday and let me tell you it was an incredible SUCCESS.

TED. Oh, happy birthday, Brett!

ANITA. It was SO. CUTE. We had all of his friends in a Zoom room and we played games and hired a magician, apparently the same magician that does the birthday parties for NPH's kids?

TED. Oh wow, he's famous.

ANITA. He really is. Now, I'll be honest with you both, I did NOT think magic would work on Zoom but I swear to God, he put a note into an apple, set the apple on fire and then took the note OUT of his MOUTH. And Brett, Brett just turned to me after and he said "Mommy, that was the best birthday I ever had" and let me tell you it broke my heart clean. In. Two. And... Patricia? Patricia, are you okay?

(**PATRICIA** *is aggressively crying.*)

TED. Oh no.

PATRICIA. I'm sorry, that story is so sweet and lovely and it's been so hard lately and I just –

I just hate magicians so much.

ANITA. Oh, sweetie, I'm sorry! We don't have to have NPH's magician.

PATRICIA. It's not that. Everything's terrible, the world is ending, I haven't left the house in weeks and then yesterday, my kids were running around the kitchen because if I let them run around they usually pass out for an hour or two in the afternoon so I can get a nap in because they're usually bursting into my room at four a.m. and jumpscaring me like the goddamn BABADOOK and I haven't gotten a full night sleep in six years so I let them run around and I'm making lunch because my partner's unemployed and has completely retreated into himself and has started making these tiny ships and putting them into even tinier bottles and can't POSSIBLY help me with the kids when all of a sudden I hear my eldest Jackie, she's six, SCREAM bloody murder and I run over to see what's wrong and I see that my youngest, David, he's four, has somehow STABBED Jackie with a FORK in her right bicep and I mean, like, STAB stabbed, like STUCK in her FLESH kind of stabbed, and while I'm standing there, trying to process this, Jackie PULLS the fork OUT of her arm and blood starts spraying EVERYWHERE and all this time David is just sitting in the corner laughing his ass off and I whirl on him, scream at him that he's a terrible child who's absolutely going to hell so then HE starts crying meanwhile I run to get the bandages and my partner's standing in the doorway with his little fucking SHIP HOBBY like "What's up?" And I knock the ship out of his hand and scream WE'RE IN A CRISIS FRED THAT'S WHAT'S UP and I drag him into the kitchen and we manage to get her arm all wrapped up and I send David to his room but what sort of punishment is that when you're trapped inside like where else is he going to go and I'm terrified because I thought I could shield my daughter from the patriarchy for a few more years, but, fuckin' NOPE her own BROTHER STABS her with a FORK and she sees how powerless I am to stop him and we're all TRAPPED in here TOGETHER and they are LUCKY that I am here to handle ANY OF THIS but I'm barely hanging on – I mean the PTA I'm supposed to run is literally just a teacher, a parent, and ME because I couldn't keep it together and if I can't keep the fucking PTA together how can I possibly keep my family together?

(**PATRICIA** *breathes, spent. A moment.*)

TED. Okay, I'm not a fast typer so, I got maybe HALF of that.

PATRICIA. I'm sorry, that was. Completely unprofessional.

ANITA. I'm sorry. Your son STABBED your daughter with a fork?

PATRICIA. Let's just move onto the next item on the agenda –

(**ANITA** *starts laughing.*)

I'm sorry, is something funny?

ANITA. I mean, YEAH.

He stabbed her with a FORK.

It's freakin' hilarious.

Kids are absolute SAVAGES.

When Brett was two, he sat on my wife's face and took a SHIT.

Right there on her face.

PATRICIA.
Jesus.

TED.
I'm not putting that in the minutes.

ANITA. It was a NIGHTMARE.

And he LAUGHED the whole time.

'Cause they don't know any better!

They're such little assholes.

We weren't SUPPOSED to ever be around them this much

That's what school was for!

My advice: throw some Midori into that morning smoothie

And seize the fuckin' DAY.

PATRICIA. Oh my God, I'm drinking too!

TED. *(Not wasted.)* Oh yeah, I'm wasted!

ANITA. See! It's great! Nothing matters! OH! I have an idea.

Sorry. I motion for a proposal: we've all got this stress just building up inside of us, so, let's give it back to the Earth. Just scream whatever's bothering us into the void of Zoom. All those in favor, say yea!

PATRICIA.
Uh –

TED.
Yea!

ANITA. The yeas have it! Go for it, Ted.

TED. I wanna be the Calculus teacher! Teaching Pre-Calc is bullshit, it's all buildup with no payoff and Derek Chambers teaches Calculus, right, and he's an incredibly sweet man, a pillar of the community and I have imagined him being killed SO many times in SO many ways, including being enveloped by lava and popping like a meat balloon.

ANITA. Ted, your creativity is SHINING today. My turn. The other day I was snooping around my oldest son Jason's room because he's at the age now where you can't find out anything unless you SNOOP, and I found a folder on his computer labeled "Secrets" and inside were just a bunch of pictures of his teachers getting fucked by horses!

TED. What? That's crazy! That's…did you delete them, or –?

PATRICIA. I HATE BEING A MOM.

TED.	**ANITA.**
Whoa.	Whoa.

PATRICIA. No, I mean, I love my kids, of course I do.

And I'm so happy they're here

But the rest of it

The actual JOB part of it

It's awful.

And I don't think we talk about that enough.

(They sit in this for a moment.)

ANITA. I have another proposal. Do we want to.

I don't know.

Meet up again next week? Not as the PTA but I dunno.

Maybe just as friends?

PATRICIA. I'd like that.

TED. Me too. Lemme just set a reminder here. And. OH. Oh no.

ANITA. What's wrong?

TED. I just accidentally sent the minutes from this meeting to the superintendent.

PATRICIA. YOU DID WHAT?!

TED. THE BUTTON ISN'T WHERE THE BUTTON SHOULD BE.

(They sit in shock. Then:)

PATRICIA. I call this meeting of the Escondido Unified School District PTA to a close, all in favor say yea.

TED.	**ANITA.**
Yea.	Yea.

PATRICIA. The yeas have it, meeting adjourned.

*(**TED** and **ANITA** leave the meeting, though it takes **TED** a bit longer. **PATRICIA** stares at her screen.)*

What if I never feel okay again?

(She clicks off.)

End of Play

www.ingramcontent.com/pod-product-compliance
Lightning Source LLC
Chambersburg PA
CBHW072012290426
44109CB00018B/2219